FOOD

OGDEN FOOD NASH

ILLUSTRATIONS BY ETIENNE DELESSERT

EDITED BY ROY FINAMORE

DESIGNED BY RITA MARSHALL

STEWART, TABORI & CHANG

NEW YORK

Published in 1989 by Stewart, Tabori & Chang, Inc.
740 Broadway, New York, New York 10003.

Library of Congress Cataloging-in-Publication Data
Nash, Ogden, 1902–1971.
   Food / Ogden Nash ; illustrations by Etienne Delessert ; edited by
Roy Finamore.
     p.   cm.
     ISBN 1-55670-062-8 : $9.95
     1. Food—Poetry.   I. Delessert, Etienne.   II. Finamore, Roy.
III. Title.
PS3527.A637A6   1989   89-30647
811'.52—dc19   CIP

Distributed in the U.S. by Workman Publishing,
708 Broadway, New York, New York 10003.

Distributed in Canada by Canadian Manda Group,
P.O. Box 920 Station U, Toronto, Ontario M8Z 5P9.

Distributed in all other territories by Little, Brown and Company,
International Division, 34 Beacon Street, Boston, Massachusetts 02108.

Printed in Japan   10 9 8 7 6 5 4 3 2 1

CONTENTS

CONTENTS

CONTENTS

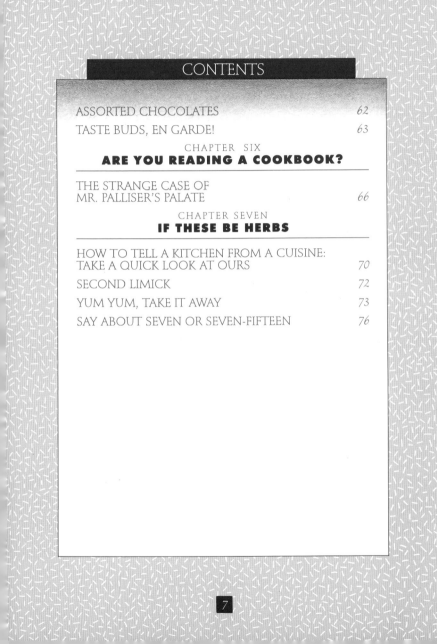

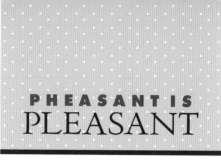

PHEASANT IS
PLEASANT

CHAPTER ONE

THE CLEAN PLATTER

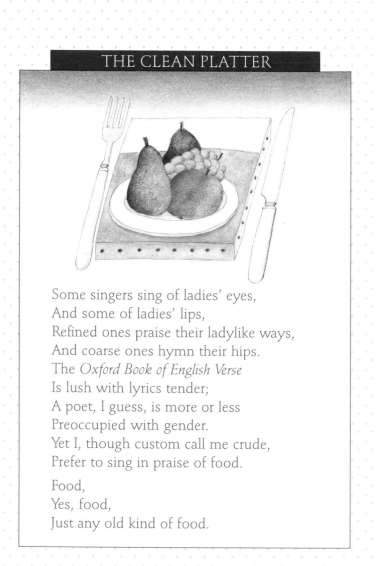

Some singers sing of ladies' eyes,
And some of ladies' lips,
Refined ones praise their ladylike ways,
And coarse ones hymn their hips.
The *Oxford Book of English Verse*
Is lush with lyrics tender;
A poet, I guess, is more or less
Preoccupied with gender.
Yet I, though custom call me crude,
Prefer to sing in praise of food.

Food,
Yes, food,
Just any old kind of food.

Pooh for the cook,
And pooh for the price!
Some of it's nicer but all of it's nice.
Pheasant is pleasant, of course,
And terrapin, too, is tasty,
Lobster I freely endorse,
In pâté or patty or pasty.
But there's nothing the matter with butter,
And nothing the matter with jam,
And the warmest of greetings I utter
To the ham and the yam and the clam.
For they're food,
All food,
And I think very highly of food.
Though I'm broody at times
When bothered by rhymes,
I brood
On food.

Some painters paint the sapphire sea,
And some the gathering storm.
Others portray young lambs at play,
But most, the female form.
'Twas trite in that primeval dawn
When painting got its start,
That a lady with her garments on

Is Life, but is she Art?
By undraped nymphs
I am not wooed;
I'd rather painters painted food.

Food,
Just food,
Just any old kind of food.
Let it be sour
Or let it be sweet,
As long as you're sure it is something to eat.
Go purloin a sirloin, my pet,
If you'd win a devotion incredible;
And asparagus tips vinaigrette,
Or anything else that is edible.
Bring salad or sausage or scrapple,
A berry or even a beet.
Bring an oyster, an egg, or an apple,
As long as it's something to eat.
If it's food,
It's food;
Never mind what kind of food.
When I ponder my mind
I consistently find
It is glued
On food.

HOLLANDAISE

I sing the praise of Hollandaise,
A sauce supreme in many ways.
Not only is it a treat to us
When ladled on asparagus,
But I would shudder to depict
A world without Eggs Benedict.

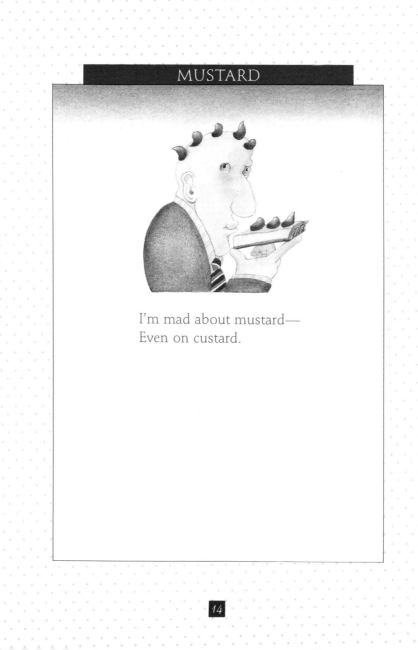

I'm mad about mustard—
Even on custard.

THE SMELT

Oh, why does man pursue the smelt?
It has no valuable pelt,
It boasts of no escutcheon royal,
It yields no ivory or oil,
Its life is dull, its death is tame,
A fish as humble as its name.
Yet—take this salmon somewhere else.
And bring me half a dozen smelts.

THE SCALLOP

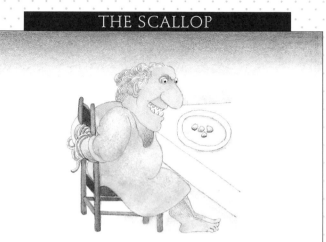

The bivalve mollusk is deemed a treat
Toward which treat-lovers hustle,
Yet it's not the scallop itself they eat,
But the scallop's adductor muscle.
My craving for pot is none of the time,
And for alcohol, sporadic,
But I cannot conceal from the scallop that I'm
An adductor muscle addic.

THE SHAD

I'm sure that Europe never had
A fish as tasty as the shad.
Some people greet the shad with groans,
Complaining of its countless bones;
I claim the bones teach table poise
And separate the men from boys.
The shad must be dissected subtle-y;
Besides, the roe is boneless, utterly.

THE CHEF HAS IMAGINATION *or* IT'S TOO HARD TO DO IT EASY

Hark to a lettuce lover.
I consider lettuce a blessing.
And what do I want on my lettuce?
Simply a simple dressing.

But in dining car and hostel
I grow apoplectic and dropsical;
Is this dressing upon my lettuce,
Or is it a melting popsicle?

A dressing is not the meal, dears,
It requires nor cream nor egg,
Nor butter nor maple sugar,
And neither the nut nor the meg.

A dressing is not a compote,
A dressing is not a custard;
It consists of pepper and salt,
Vinegar, oil, and mustard.

It is not paprika and pickles,
Let us leave those to the Teutons;
It is not a pinkish puddle
Of grenadine and Fig Newtons.

Must I journey to France for dressing?
It isn't a baffling problem;
Just omit the molasses and yoghurt,
The wheat germ, and the Pablum.

It's oil and vinegar, dears,
No need to tiddle and toil;
Just salt and pepper and mustard,
And vinegar, and oil.

For Brillat-Savarin, then, and Hoyle,
Stick, friends, to vinegar and oil!
Yachtsman, jettison boom and spinnaker,
Bring me oil and bring me vinegar!
Play the music of Haydn or Honegger,
But lace it with honest oil and vinegar!
Choir in church or mosque or synagogue,
Sing, please, in praise of oil and vinegogue.
I'm not an expert, just a beginneger,
But I place my trust in oil and vinegar.
May they perish, as Remus was perished
    by Romulus,
Who monkey with this, the most sacred
    of formulas.

I'LL TAKE
A BUN

CHAPTER TWO

ICEBERG LETTUCE

I cheerfully forgive my debtors,
But I'll never pardon iceberg lettuce,
A pallid package of rigidity,
A globe of frozen insipidity.
I hope I'll never be so punchy
As to relish my salad crisp and crunchy,
Yet garden lettuce with leafy head
Is as hard to get as unsliced bread.

In mortal combat I am joined
With monstrous words wherever coined
"Beefburger" is a term worth hating,
Both fraudulent and infuriating,
Contrived to foster the belief
That only beefburgers are made of beef,
Implying with shoddy flim and flam
That hamburgers are made of ham.

I'd like to be able to say a good word for parsley,
but I can't,

And after all what can you find to say for something that even the dictionary dismisses as a biennial umbelliferous plant?

Speaking of which, I don't know how the dictionary figures it as biennial, it is biennial my eye, it is like the poor and the iniquitous,

Because it is always with us, because it is permanent and ubiquitous.

I will not venture to deny that it is umbelliferous,

I will only add that it is of a nasty green color, and faintly odoriferous,

And I hold by my complaint, though every cook

and hostess in the land indict me for treason
for it,
That parsley is something that as a rhymer I can
find no rhyme for it and as an eater I can find
no reason for it.
Well, there is one sin for which a lot of cooks and
hostesses are some day going to have to atone,
Which is that they can't bear to cook anything
and leave it alone.
No, they see food as something to base a lot of
beautiful dreams and romance on,
Which explains lamb chops with pink and blue
pants on.
Everything has to be all decorated and garnished
So the guests will be amazed and astarnished,
And whatever you get to eat, it's sprinkled with a
lot of good old umbelliferous parsley looking
as limp and wistful as Lillian Gish,
And it is limpest, and wistfulest, and also thick-
est, on fish.
Indeed, I think maybe one reason for the disap-
pearance of Enoch Arden
Was that his wife had an idea that mackerel
tasted better if instead of looking like mackerel
it looked like a garden.

Well, anyhow, there's the parsley cluttering up
   your food,
And the problem is to get it off without being
   rude,
And first of all you try to scrape it off with your
   fork,
And you might as well try to shave with a cork,
And then you surreptitiously try your fingers,
And you get covered with butter and gravy, but
   the parsley lingers,
And you turn red and smile at your hostess and
   compliment her on the recipe and ask her
   where she found it,
And then you return to the parsley and as a last
   resort you try to eat around it,
And the hostess says, Oh you are just picking at
   it, is there something wrong with it?
So all you can do is eat it all up, and the parsley
   along with it,
And now is the time for all good parsleyphobes
   to come to the aid of the menu and exhibit
   their gumption,
And proclaim that any dish that has either a taste
   or an appearance that can be improved by
   parsley is *ipso facto* a dish unfit for human
   consumption.

THE PARSNIP

The parsnip, children, I repeat
Is simply an anemic beet.
Some people call the parsnip edible;
Myself, I find this claim incredible.

THE CARAWAY SEED

The Abbé Voltaire, alias Arouet,
Never denounced the seed of the caraway;
Sufficient proof, if proof we need,
That he never bit into a caraway seed.

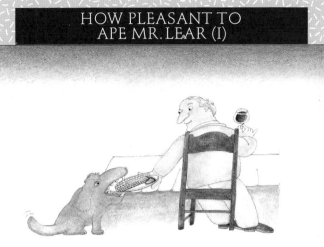

The Pilgrims ate quahaugs and corn yet,
Which gourmets would scorn through a
    lorgnette.
    For this kind of living
    They proclaimed a Thanksgiving.
I'm thankful I hadn't been born yet.

THE SWEETBREAD

That sweetbread gazing up at me
Is not what it purports to be.
Says Webster in one paragraph,
It is the pancreas of a calf.
Since it is neither sweet nor bread,
I think I'll take a bun instead.

THE CODFISH

The codfish is a staple food
For which I'm seldom in the mood.
This fish is such an utter loss
That people eat it with egg sauce,
One of the odd fish codfish habits
I leave to the Lowells and the Cabots.

A gourmet challenged me to eat
A tiny bit of rattlesnake meat,
Remarking, "Don't look horror-stricken,
You'll find it tastes a lot like chicken."
It did.
Now chicken I cannot eat.
Because it tastes like rattlesnake meat.

THE POMEGRANATE

The hardest fruit upon this planet
Is easily the ripe pomegranate.
I'm halfway through the puzzle game
Of guessing how it got its name.
The pome part turns my cowlick hoary,
But the granite is self-explanatory.

There are certain people
Whom certain herbs
The good digestion of disturbs.
Henry VIII
Divorced Catherine of Aragon
Because of her reckless use of tarragon.

Parsley
Is gharsley.

MEN ARE
GLUTTONS

CHAPTER THREE

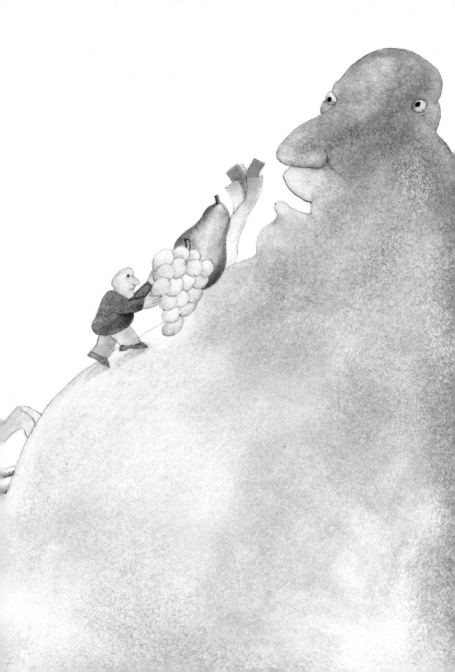

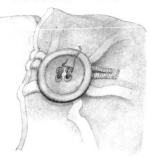

Man is a glutton,
He will eat too much even though there be
    nothing to eat much of but parsnips or
    mutton.
He will deprecate his paunch,
And immediately afterwards reach for another
    jowl or haunch.
People don't have to be Cassandras or Catos
To know what will happen to their paunches if
    they combine hot biscuits and strawberry
    shortcake and French fried potatoes,

Yet no sooner has a man achieved a one-pound loss

Than he gains two through the application to an old familiar dish or a new irresistible sauce.

Thus cooks aggravate men's gluttony

With capers and hollandaise and chutney,

They can take seaweed or pemmican

And do things to them in a ramekin,

Give them a gopher that has perished of exposure

And they will whip you up a casserole of ambrosia,

Which is why a man who digs his grave with his teeth's idea of life beyond the grave is definite,

There's a divine chef in it.

Men are gluttons,

And everybody knows it except tailors, who don't leave room enough at the edge to move over the buttons.

WHICH CAME FIRST,
OBEISANCE OR OBESITY?

You'd be sitting pretty, with nothing in the world
  to trouble you,
Were it not that someone quite high up in your
  family is quite high up in the I.O.O.P.W.,
So at mealtime your heart with apprehension is
  filled,
Because the I.O.O.P.W. is the International Order
  of Plate Watchers—a powerful and articulate
  guild.
A Plate Watcher, I need hardly state,
Watches everybody else's plate.
She begins with over-hospitality

And ends up with aggressive frugality.

She urges people to help themselves far beyond their capacity, to pile mashed potatoes on Yorkshire pudding, and apple pandowdy on shoofly pie,

And then fixes them with a waste-not, want-not eye.

She smelleth the laggard afar off; she saith among the diners, Ha, ha!

And woe betide him who has attempted to conceal beneath the cutlery one ultimate tiny little *petit pois*.

Indeed, woe doubly betides that reluctant regaler,

For he has been ordered to watch his weight by both his physician and, what is more important, his tailor.

I recommend to any ardent debate watcher

A seat at table presided over by a Plate Watcher married to a weight watcher.

IT'S THE
LIQUOR

CHAPTER FOUR

In Duluth there's a hostess, forsooth,
Who doesn't know gin from vermouth,
But this lubricant lapse
Isn't noticed, perhaps
Because nobody does in Duluth.

Candy
Is dandy
But liquor
Is quicker.

SING A SONG OF TASTE BUDS

The wine snob is so well established,
His clichés are so widely published,
He's so ingenuous in his worship
Of his own erudite connoisseurship,
He gives himself such harmless pleasure
That you humor him in modest measure
And sometimes ask him how to tell
An honest from a great Moselle,
As one who tosses from his rocker
A ball to please an eager cocker.
To paraphrase Aesop's pithy parlarance,
Familiarity breeds tolerance.

The gin snob, on the other hand,
Has lately burst upon the land.
More brash than the oenologist
Who judges grapes, he judges grist,
Presumably grading in his brain
The varying vintage years of grain.
This man of the world can find no merit
In any domestic neutral spirit.
No Kansas maidens, skirts a-ripple,
Shall tread the kernels for his tipple,
Nebraska, no, nor Ioway,
Provide it body and bouquet;
The gin employed to make him squiffy
Must be distilled near Thames or Liffey.
His own, his native strong drink he mocks,
Demanding Old Hogarth on the rocks
Until tomorrow or next week
Old Muttoneater becomes more chic.

I prefer a twice-told tale of vineyards
To a guided tour through alien ginyards.

There is something about a martini,
A tingle remarkably pleasant;
A yellow, a mellow martini;
I wish that I had one at present.
There is something about a martini,
Ere the dining and dancing begin,
And to tell you the truth,
It is not the vermouth—
I think that perhaps it's the gin.

There is something about an old-fashioned
That kindles a cardiac glow;
It is soothing and soft and impassioned
As a lyric by Swinburne or Poe.
There is something about an old-fashioned
When dusk has enveloped the sky,
And it may be the ice,
Or the pineapple slice,
But I strongly suspect it's the rye.

There is something about a mint julep.

It is nectar imbibed in a dream,
As fresh as the bud of the tulip,
As cool as the bed of the stream.
There is something about a mint julep,
A fragrance beloved by the lucky.
And perhaps it's the tint
Of the frost and the mint,
But I think it was born in Kentucky.

There is something they put in a highball
That awakens the torpidest brain,
That kindles a spark in the eyeball,
Gliding singing through vein after vein.
There is something they put in a highball
Which you'll notice one day, if you watch;
And it may be the soda,
But judged by the odor,
I rather believe it's the scotch.

Then here's to the heartening wassail,
Wherever good fellows are found;
Be its master instead of its vassal,
And order the glasses around.
For there's something they put in the wassail
That prevents it from tasting like wicker;
Since it's not tapioca,
Or mustard, or mocha,
I'm forced to conclude it's the liquor.

CELERY
RAW

CHAPTER 5

The calf is born with prospects grim,
His life will not be kind to him.
It holds no weal, but only woe,
At home as veal, in France as *veau*.

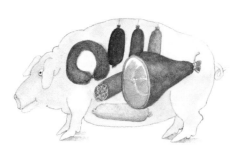

The pig, if I am not mistaken,
Supplies us sausage, ham, and bacon.
Let others say his heart is big—
I call it stupid of the pig.

THE SQUAB

Toward a better world I contribute my
    modest smidgin;
I eat the squab, lest it become a pigeon.

I seek in anonymity's cloister
Not him who ate the first raw oyster,
But one who, braving spikes and prickles,
The spine that stabs, the leaf that tickles,
With infinite patience and fortitude
Unveiled the artichoke as food.

YORKSHIRE PUDDING

Let us call Yorkshire pudding
A fortunate blunder;
It's a sort of popover
That tripped and popped under.

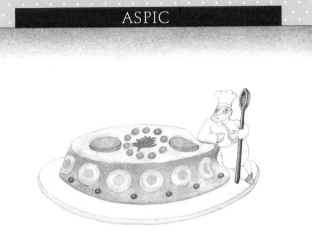

What a pity that aspic
Doesn't rhyme with elastic,
Because gee whiz,
It is.

Celery, raw,
Develops the jaw,
But celery, stewed,
Is more quickly chewed.

Sea horses may be Romanized
By calling them hippocampi;
If you would do the same to shrimp,
Add garlic and they're scampi.

THE KIPPER

For half a century, man and nipper,
I've doted on a tasty kipper,
But since I am no Jack the Ripper
I wish the kipper had a zipper.

THE CANTALOUPE

One cantaloupe is ripe and lush,
Another's green, another's mush.
I'd buy a lot more cantaloupe
If I possessed a fluoroscope.

If some confectioner were willing
To let the shape announce the filling,
We'd encounter fewer assorted chocs,
Bitten into and returned to the box.

Although I'll eat the strawberry when frozen
It's not the very berry I'd have chosen.
The naughty admen claim with gall divine
That it is better than the genu-ine,
New language they devise to sing its praise,
But only *le bon Dieu* can coin a *fraise*.

ARE YOU READING A COOKBOOK?

CHAPTER SIX

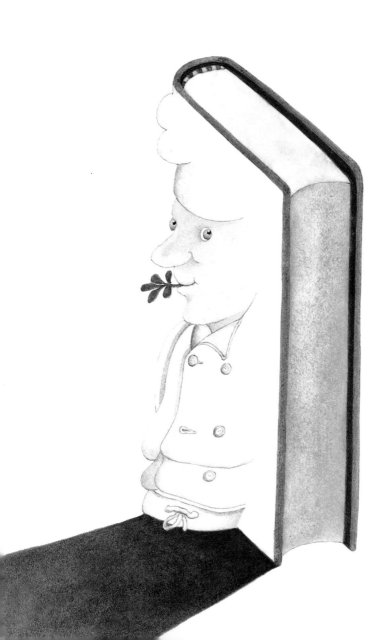

THE STRANGE CASE
OF MR. PALLISER'S PALATE

Once there was a man named Mr. Palliser and he
 asked his wife, May I be a *gourmet*?
And she said, You sure may,
But she also said, If my kitchen is going to pro-
 duce a Cordon Blue,
It won't be me, it will be you,
And he said, You mean *Cordon Bleu*?
And she said to never mind the pronunciation so
 long as it was him and not *heu*.
But he wasn't discouraged; he bought a white
 hat and *The Cordon Bleu Cook Book* and said,
 How about some *Huîtres en Robe de Chambre*?
And she sniffed and said, Are you reading a
 cookbook or Forever *Ambre*?

And he said, Well, if you prefer something more Anglo-Saxon,

Why suppose I whip up some tasty *Filets de Sole Jackson*,

And she pretended not to hear, so he raised his voice and said, Could I please you with some *Paupiettes de Veau à la Grecque* or *Cornets de Jambon Lucullus* or perhaps some nice *Moules à la Bordelaise*?

And she said, Kindly lower your voice or the neighbors will think we are drunk and *dis-ordelaise*,

And she said, Furthermore the whole idea of your cooking anything fit to eat is a farce. So what did Mr. Palliser do then?

Well, he offered her *Oeufs Farcis Maison* and *Homard Farci St. Jacques* and *Tomate Farcie à la Bayonne* and *Aubergines Farcies Provençales*, as well as *Aubergines Farcies Italiennes*,

And she said, Edward, kindly accompany me as usual to Hamburger Heaven and stop playing the fool,

And he looked in the book for one last suggestion and it suggested *Croques Madame*, so he did, and now he dines every evening on *Crème de Concombres Glacée, Côtelettes de Volaille Vicomtesse*, and *Artichauds à la Barigoule*.

IF THESE BE HERBS

CHAPTER SEVEN

HOW TO TELL A KITCHEN FROM A CUISINE: TAKE A QUICK LOOK AT OURS

Every time the menu lists *bleu* cheese I want to order *fromage* blue,

Don't you?

Yet when they call it *bleu* cheese I suppose they are right,

Because *bleu* cheese differs from blue cheese because it is usually white.

I must read up on this matter in the cheese cook book,

Which clutters up our kitchen along with the fish cook book, the game cook book, the wine cook book, the Colonial cook book, the French cook book, the Eskimo cook book and the Siamese cook book.

Yes, in our kitchen there are everywhere you look books,

There may be a stove, but you can't see the cook box for the cook books.

You know the way some larders are full of pota-
toes and lentils and beans?
That's the way ours is full of recipes clipped from
newspapers and magazines.
Having perused this mass of culinariana I have
one hope that is definite;
I hope we will always have a kitchen, but I hope I
will never be the chef in it,
Because my few attempts to emulate Clemen-
tine Paddleford or Brillat-Savarin,
They have resulted in results something less than
mouth-waterin', or -slaverin'.
If there is one element of cookery I deplore,
It is that when you go to cook, the recipe sud-
denly calls for a roux or a stock or something
that should have been started the day before.
I attribute the brilliance of Gian-Carlo Menotti
To the fact that he has never tasted my manicotti,
Because my ignorance is so profound
That I don't know whether manicotti should be
rectangular or round.
In this respect even my limited knowledge of
money is preciser;
I know that the round kind is nice but the rec-
tangular kind is much nicer.

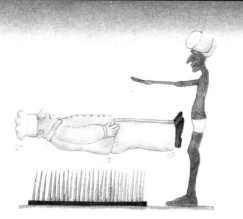

A cook named McMurray
Got a raise in a hurry
From his Hindu employer
By favoring curry.

9 7822463 3357

Do you wonder why, when you sit down to eat,
 you start twisting in your chair and drumming
 on the table with your digits?
Because of dysphoria, which is a state of dissatis-
 faction, anxiety, restlessness or the fidgets,
Which is caused by anticipation of dysphagia, or
 difficulty in swallowing,
Which is caused by two hazards of dining with
 friends today, namely, the following:
Hazard number one is the hostess who fan-
 cies herself as a gourmet, or should I say
 gourmette;
Hers is a table at which even between courses
 you first take out and then hastily put back
 your cigarette.

When does a housewife blossom into a Brillat-
    Savarin? I will tell you when;
It is when she has a newspaper or magazine
    clipping, a clove of garlic, and a Rock Cornish
    hen.
Herbs are another status symbol, so as you
    work your way through the tossed epicurean
    forage,
Why, you are supposed to detect and appreciate
    the difference between the oregano and the
    saxifrage, and the chervil and the borage.
Frankly, I don't know whether I'd less rather eat
    them or guess them;
If these be Herbs, I'm willing for Herb to re-
    possess them.
Hazard number two is no gourmet, she is the
    backbone of the economy in this land of the
    free;
This hostess serves nothing that isn't displayed
    wrapped in cellophane at the supermarket ex-
    actly as advertised on her TV.
Even before by the first mouthful your palate is
    mortified
You know you will be confronted with sub-
    stances presliced, processed, tenderized, poly-
    unsaturated, dehydrated, or fortified.

You are in an evil humor;

If, as Sir Winston has said, the good is the enemy of the best, so is the just-as-good the enemy of the bemused consumer.

This truth is so evident that even the advertiser will occasionally resort to it as a final expedient;

Witness the less expensive spread that is promoted as better than other less expensive spreads because it boasts of containing some of the more expensive spread as an ingredient.

You know your desire is foolhardy, it is the essence of foolhardihoodness,

But you desire to eat something that tastes like something, rather than something you are told will zestfully stimulate your taste buds with its mouth-watering goodness.

Which last is an eventuality not to be trifled with;

I heard of one consumer who consumed a product so mouth-watering that his taste buds got over-mouth-watered and grew to the size of chrysanthemums, which he was stifled with.

This is the only exception I can give

To the paradoxical rule that the more insipid and unappetizing our diet, the longer we seem to live.

A super party is something at which you arrive
either long before or long after the rest of the
competitors,

And you broke your glasses on the way over
and can't tell people you know from people
you don't know or your creditors from your
debitors,

And you had thought your morning shave would
see you through and you suddenly realize that
your chin is growing shadowy, not to say
tufty.

And you discover that you are either the only
male in evening clothes or the only one in
mufti,

And as if your spirits were not by now suffi-
ciently dankish,

Well, you also discover that you alone didn't
    know it was a birthday party and are the only
    arrival not to bring in a package either useful
    or prankish,
But with the arrival of the cocktails your spirits
    are turned from the swath and scattered for
    drying, or as the crossword puzzlers put it,
    tedded,
Until you realize with a shudder that you re-
    ceived through an error the cocktail specially
    mixed by the host for his brother-in-law, who
    is notoriously light-headed,
And you choke it down, and not till the salad is
    served do you recover from your croup,
At which point it seems that you have no fork
    left, the implication being either that it now
    rests in your pocket or that you used two forks
    on your soup.
But it is only later that the earth really begins to
    spin like a fretful midge,
When it transpires that in this gathering of eight
    or twelve or sixteen it is you and you alone by
    yourself who do not play bridge.
You may well echo the words of the poet as you
    eventually wend your homeward way.
"Fate," said the poet firmly, "cannot harm me
    further, I have dined today."

DESIGNED BY RITA MARSHALL

COMPOSED IN STEMPEL SCHNEIDLER LIGHT
AND FUTURA EXTRA BLACK
BY TRUFONT TYPOGRAPHERS, INC.,
HICKSVILLE, NEW YORK.

PRINTED AND BOUND BY
TOPPAN PRINTING COMPANY, LTD.,
TOKYO, JAPAN.